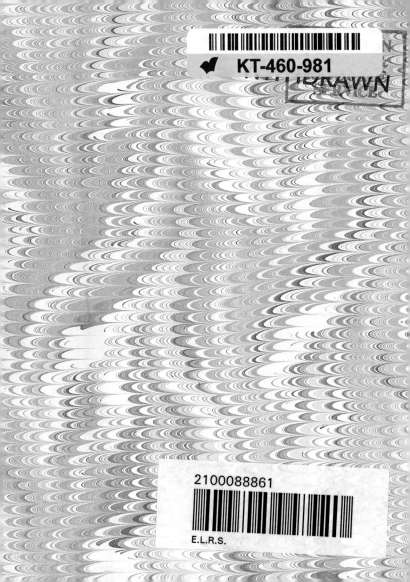

THE NATIONAL TRUST
Little Library

SWEET
Flavourings

JILL NORMAN

DORLING KINDERSLEY
LONDON

EDITOR GWEN EDMONDS

DESIGNER JOANNA MARTIN

PHOTOGRAPHER DAVE KING

ART DIRECTOR STUART JACKMAN

FIRST PUBLISHED IN GREAT BRITAIN IN 1989 BY
DORLING KINDERSLEY LIMITED
9 HENRIETTA STREET, LONDON WC2E 8PS

BRITISH LIBRARY CATALOGUING IN PUBLICATION DATA

NORMAN, JILL
FLAVOURINGS
THE NATIONAL TRUST LITTLE LIBRARY
I. FOOD. FLAVOURINGS
I. TITLE II. SERIES
641. 338

ISBN 0-86318-304-2

PRINTED AND BOUND
IN HONG KONG BY IMAGO

CONTENTS

INTRODUCTION

CREATING FLAVOUR *is one of the most important elements of good cooking. A bowl of porridge may be filling, but it would be a dull thing if cooked without salt or served without cream or milk and maybe a spoonful of honey.*

Some flavourings are used to develop the taste of other ingredients, others add their own distinctive character to a dish. The success of a dish often comes from adding tiny amounts of an unusual flavouring, but to do this you need experience as well as imagination. The exact amount of a flavouring needed in any recipe is almost impossible to determine, so much depends upon individual taste and on the

Spanish lemon wrapper

ingredients which will vary from place to place and from day to day. 'Season to taste' should mean just what it says: it is best to taste a dish while it is cooking and again at the end to make sure the flavour is what it is meant to be.

This book concentrates on flavourings we usually associate with sweet dishes, although there are also recipes for meat and vegetables and 'savoury' preserves. The blending of sweet and sour was common in European cooking until the 17th century and is still found, albeit in very different styles, in China and in parts of the Middle East and North Africa.

Nuts are an important flavouring throughout the lands that stretch from North Africa to Afghanistan. They occur in sauces, meat and fish dishes, pilafs and pastries, giving texture as well as flavour to the food.

Vanilla and chocolate were brought from America by the Spaniards. The Aztecs already used vanilla as a flavouring for chocolate. Both are now widely used to give their distinctive flavours to many other foods – vanilla in cold soups, chocolate in traditional Mexican *mole* sauces for poultry, both of them in countless desserts and items of confectionery.

Citrus fruits offer the most versatile range of flavourings worldwide. Dried tangerine peel is used in Chinese stir-fried dishes; in Provence a strip of orange peel is one of the flavourings for a slow-cooked *daube* of beef; West Indians use Seville orange juice in cooking meat and poultry; in South America and around the Pacific fish to be eaten raw is marinated in lemon or lime juice; Moroccans preserve lemons in salt; in India pickled limes are a favourite.

This little book shows you how these flavourings are used in cuisines around the world and some ways they have been used by cooks in the past. There is inspiration here to add an extra dimension to both sweet and savoury dishes.

CHOCOLATE

*C*HOCOLATE IS MADE *from the beans of the cacao tree* (Theobroma cacao), *cultivated since ancient times in tropical South America and the West Indies, and later introduced to West Africa, Ceylon and Indonesia.*

Unsweetened cooking chocolate

Bitter chocolate

The beans are contained in the pulp of large elliptical pods. They are separated out, often after some fermentation, roasted and crushed, and the kernels split into irregular-shaped cocoa nibs. The Mexicans made a drink called *xocolatl* from cakes of roast ground kernels which the Spaniards introduced to Europe around 1520. The drink was fairly acid so sugar was added and the cakes often contained a mixture of spices such as cinnamon and vanilla.

Milk chocolate

Cocoa powder

White chocolate

hardened, is *UNSWEETENED COOKING CHOCOLATE* – the basic chocolate liquor, sold in tablets.

BITTER CHOCOLATE is the most basic form in which eating chocolate is sold in bars and blocks.

MILK CHOCOLATE, developed in the 1870s and originally made with condensed milk, is not very suitable for cooking.

COCOA POWDER can be used for flavour, but to obtain a true chocolate effect must be enriched with butter (up to half its own weight) and sugar.

COUVERTURE is a confectioners' chocolate with a very high cocoa butter content that makes it very tricky to use.

WHITE 'CHOCOLATE' is a confection of cocoa butter, milk and sugar which does not contain any chocolate liquor.

CHOCOLATE-FLAVOURED COVERINGS are wholly artificial and therefore best avoided.

Later ready-to-use cocoa powder and cocoa paste were manufactured.

Cocoa nibs consist for half their weight of cocoa butter. Ground to a paste, with varying proportions of cocoa butter, the nibs become the chocolate liquor which, when

CITRUS FRUITS

Bear me, Pomona! to thy citron groves
To where the lemon and the piercing lime,
With the deep orange glowing through the green
Their lighter glories blend.

James Thomson, The seasons, 1727

THE GENUS CITRUS to which all the citrus fruits belong originated in China and India and forms the largest and most important group of tropical and sub-tropical fruit. They seem to have been known in Europe from about 300 BC, and earlier in Persia and Mesopotamia. Certainly lemons and limes were known to the Romans, but it was the Arabs who propagated citrus fruit around the Mediterranean and it was Columbus who took them across the Atlantic. The many members of the genus are all evergreen trees, their fruit varies in size, shape and colour, but holds a common attraction: a very high concentration of sugars and acids (including ascorbic acid or vitamin C) in the juice. Sugar dominates in most of them, making them pleasant to eat fresh.

Orange tree

Where the acids have the upper hand, as in lime or lemon, they dictate other ways of using the fruit. As flavourings their most important part is the essential oil which is principally in the skin. This may be taken by rubbing the skin with a lump of sugar, by grating it very finely, or by removing it with a zester. The peel itself may be candied or used fresh. Pectin, used in making jam, is another citrus product.

C I T R O N

*C*ITRUS MEDICA *was probably the first citrus fruit to come west, or may even have originated in the Arabian peninsula. It was cultivated in Persia and is thought to have reached Babylon even before its conquest by Cyrus in 538 BC: the Hebrews he allowed to go home may have taken it to Palestine. Whether it was already grown in the Hanging Gardens which Nebuchadrezzar established in the 12th century BC is a matter of speculation.*

Citron had reached the Mediterranean around 300 BC, when Theophrastus mentioned it, and virtually the whole of its European cultivation still takes place in Greece, Sicily and Corsica. It also grows well in the West Indies where the Spanish colonists introduced it; Cuba and Puerto Rico are the great New World producers. The citron tree is small, seldom more than about 10 feet (3 metres), but its fruit is quite large, a rough-skinned yellow object shaped like a lemon or pear and up to 8 inches (20 cm) long. It has a very thick inner skin and a rather acid pulp.

Culinary use of the citron is limited mostly to its peel, which is candied by soaking in brine and preserving in sugar. Its taste is almost resinous by comparison with the other citrus peels. The United States is the main importer. Oil extracted from the skin is sometimes used to flavour liqueurs but is more often found in perfumes.

Citron

LEMON & LIME

THE LEMON (CITRUS LIMON) *was known in the* Middle East and Egypt before the Arab conquests, and Columbus took the lemon to the New World on his second voyage in 1493.

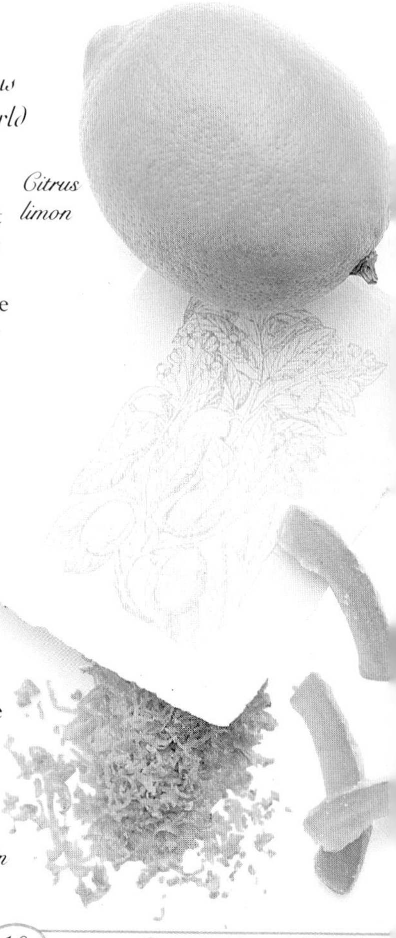

Citrus limon

The lemon tree averages about 13–17 feet (4–5 metres) and is the most decorative of the citrus trees: spiny, bearing pale green leaves and bright yellow fruit. It is widely grown in subtropical climates, but the Mediterranean and California are its main commercial producers.

The lemon has a high concentration of citric acid in the pulp which makes it unsuitable for eating as a fruit, but the juice gives a pleasant sharp flavour to many dishes and drinks. It can also be used to counter the greasy or oily effect of other foods, as a lively alternative to vinegar in dressings, and as a souring agent.

Grated lemon skin

The finely grated skin is used in baking and confectionery, and twists of skin or slices of the fruit enliven many drinks. *Citrus aurantifolia* probably originated in southern India but today limes are cultivated throughout the tropics. The lime tree is shrubby and seldom more than about 12 feet (4 metres). Its fruit is light green, and usually no wider than 1½ inches (4 cm).

The cooking of the West Indies and Mexico is unthinkable without the lime, and it is particularly good in mixed drinks. It is seldom possible to substitute lemon for lime, for their flavours are quite different, lime is very sour indeed, with a hint of bitterness absent in lemons.

Candied lemon peel

Lime

O R A N G E

ITTER ORANGES (C. AURANTIUM) came from the southern slopes of the Himalayas, and were brought west from India by the Arabs reaching Spain in the 10th century. From the orange groves planted in southern Spain they still have their popular name of Seville oranges, and Spain is still their main producer.

Far too astringent to be eaten as a fruit, most bitter oranges go into the production of marmalade but as a flavouring their highly aromatic peel deserves to be better known. The equally strongly scented flowers are used for orange flower water, jams and perfumes. Bergamot oranges (*C. bergamia*) are a variety of bitter orange cultivated for their oil, an important perfume ingredient and the flavourant of Earl Grey's tea.

Sweet oranges (*C. sinensis*) came to Europe from the Far East in the 16th century; the Spaniards took them to the New World, and by 1565 they were established in Florida. The sweet orange tree grows in any warm climate, and its commercial exploitation takes place in sub-tropical or Mediterranean-type regions. Blood oranges are a very sweet

Sweet orange

variety with dark red juice.
Navel oranges, are a seedless
variety with a navel-like blunt
apex. Most sweet oranges are
eaten fresh or used for their
juice, but the skin contains
a flavouring oil with many
culinary applications, and
is the basis of a
number of liqueurs
such as Cointreau,
and Grand Marnier.

Navel orange

Blood orange

Candied orange peel

KUMQUAT &
TANGERINE

*I*TS APPEARANCE *as a miniature orange notwithstanding, the kumquat is not a member of the citrus family at all, but a shrub of the genus* Fortunella *(named after Robert Fortune who presented a plant to the Royal Horticultural Society in 1846). It is not much grown outside China.*

The fruit has a sour taste and is seldom eaten fresh, but used pickled or candied. The skin is rich in a pungent oil which can be used for flavouring.

Kumquat

Clementine

Citrus reticulata consists of a bewildering number of varieties made more baffling by the indiscriminate use of names.

Tangerines look rather like a medium orange flattened at top and bottom. They are sweet and highly scented, with a dark orange skin that is loose and easy to detach. Mandarin oranges are lighter in colour and tighter in the skin, but otherwise similar.

Satsumas are a variety developed in Japan, small and usually seedless.

Clementines are a hybrid between tangerine and bitter orange, and midway between the two in colour, taste and ease of peeling.

All these fruits are mostly eaten fresh, but they can be put to good use in baking and cooking. Both the juice and the oil are very pungent. In China dried tangerine peel is used as a flavouring.

Satsuma

Tangerine

Dried tangerine peel

ALMOND

P RUNUS AMYGDALUS *is a native of the Near East now grown in many warm temperate climates, such as the Mediterranean, western Asia, California and southern Australia. It is the dominant nut in world trade.*

Sweet almonds

Flaked almonds

Ground almonds

Blanched almonds

The almond is a small tree resembling the peach, but the fruit is smaller and inedible when ripe. Very young, with the stone still soft, it is pleasantly sour and can be eaten, usually with a little salt. Ground sweet almonds (var. *dulcis*) are a thickening flavourant in soups and meat stews, are mixed with flour for pastry, and marzipan and almond paste are made of

them. Flaked almonds do well in salads or with fish. Roast almonds have a different flavour from fresh ones, and fried nuts are used in India and Pakistan as well as in Spain.

The bitter almond (var. *amara*) is used to make flavouring essences. A mildly nutty oil, obtained by pressing, either type of almond can be used as a cooking or salad oil.

COCONUT

*T*HE COCONUT PALM (COCOS NUCIFERA) *flourishes in tropical lowlands especially near the seashores, the light but impermeable fruit being quite often distributed by sea. Every part of the coconut palm is used but the fruit has the most uses of all.*

Desiccated coconut

Grated coconut

Coconut

The fibrous husk yields coir for cord, mats and brushes. The nut inside is what we know as a coconut. Its flesh is eaten fresh or dried (copra), the milky juice is a refreshing drink. Coconut oil, pressed or boiled from the copra, separates into a solid used for candles and a liquid used in the manufacture of cosmetics and margarine.

In the West, coconut as a flavouring is mostly confined to the flaked desiccated flesh, used, sometimes toasted, in baking or in desserts. In the East it is far more widely used, mainly in the form of 'coconut milk' or 'cream', made by macerating finely shredded flesh and pressing out the liquid.

O T H E R N U T S

Marron glacé

Roasted chestnuts

CHESTNUTS (Castanea sativa) *are very large trees, often over 100 feet (30 metres) high. Natives of southern Europe, they are now cultivated in many other temperate climates, both for timber and for nuts.*
The nuts are eaten whole (boiled, roasted or preserved in syrup) or used ground as a flavourful thickening for soups and stews or in stuffings.

HAZEL or cob nuts (Corylus avellana) *grow on small bushy trees which were found wild in Asia Minor, Europe and North America and which have provided man with food since mesolithic times.*

Hazelnuts

Walnuts

WALNUTS (Juglans regia) *grew throughout the temperate zones of Europe and Asia, while black walnuts* (Juglans nigra) *were native to North America. Both are very large trees, often cultivated for their timber. Young walnuts picked green are good in salads, pickled, or preserved in syrup. Mature nuts are used (whole, broken or ground) in stuffings, sauces, stews, and in baking. Walnut oil is an expensive but excellent salad oil.*

Pecans

*PECAN NUTS (*Carya illinoensis*) and those of other hickories native to North America are closely related to the walnut and have similar uses.*

Pine nuts

*PEANUTS (*Arachis hypogaea*) are not nuts at all, but the beans of a South American legume now grown in most subtropical climates. Their oil is one of the best cooking oils and does not disgrace a salad either. Roasted peanuts and peanut butter are important in many southeast Asian and Indonesian sauces. Peanut butter is used in North American baking.*

PINE NUTS are the kernels of Pinus pinea, *the stone pine, a native of the Mediterranean region. Their delicate flavour virtually disappears with heating, but is appreciated in stuffings and in sweet dishes. Their best known use is in pesto sauce.*

Peanuts

*PISTACHIO (*Pistacia vera*) is an evergreen tree probably native to Iran but now widely cultivated. The kernel is green, rich and oily, with a red outer skin, they are used, to make ice cream, flavour nougat and pastries.*

Pistachios

S U G A R

*S*UGAR CANE (SACCHARUM OFFICINARUM) *is a tall perennial grass with erect solid succulent stems. It has been cultivated in tropical Asia long enough for its country of origin to be obscure and by the 10th century had been brought west by the Arabs. Sugar extraction from the juice is a complicated and now highly mechanized process. Cane sugar accounts for over half the world's sugar supply.*

Sugar beet (*Beta vulgaris*) has been the source of sugar in temperate zones since the early 19th century. Its exploitation in Europe began with Napoleon's boycott of British-controlled imports of sugar cane. The United States and Russia both produce huge quantities. Beet sugar is indistinguishable from cane. Sugar is available in a variety of forms, differing mostly as to the degree of refinement.

MUSCOVADO SUGAR is raw cane sugar rich in molasses

JAGGERY is a form of raw light brown lump sugar much used in India

DEMERARA was raw cane sugar in the form of large crystals, but in commerce today is

Granulated sugar

Cube sugar

Icing sugar

Coffee sugar

Yellow rock sugar

Muscovado

Barbados sugar

Demerara

usually refined sugar mixed with molasses

BARBADOS SUGAR is made from the residual syrup after white sugar has been refined out

COFFEE SUGAR has large crystals which dissolve slowly

PRESERVING SUGAR is large crystal sugar which dissolves slowly

GRANULATED SUGAR is almost pure sucrose

CUBE SUGAR is granulated sugar moistened and moulded

CASTER SUGAR is similar to granulated but has much smaller crystals

ICING SUGAR is ground white sugar

YELLOW ROCK SUGAR is a Chinese confection of raw brown sugar, honey and granulated sugar

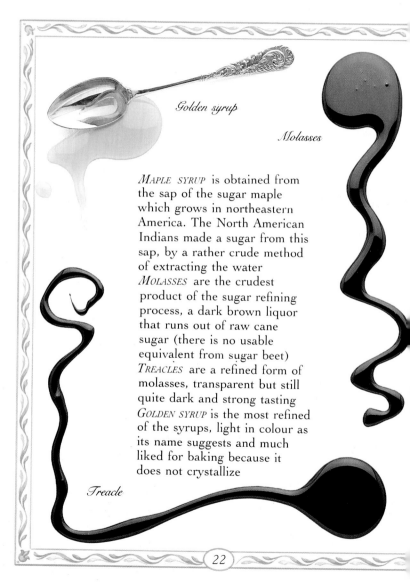

Golden syrup

Molasses

MAPLE SYRUP is obtained from the sap of the sugar maple which grows in northeastern America. The North American Indians made a sugar from this sap, by a rather crude method of extracting the water *MOLASSES* are the crudest product of the sugar refining process, a dark brown liquor that runs out of raw cane sugar (there is no usable equivalent from sugar beet) *TREACLES* are a refined form of molasses, transparent but still quite dark and strong tasting *GOLDEN SYRUP* is the most refined of the syrups, light in colour as its name suggests and much liked for baking because it does not crystallize

Treacle

HONEY

*H*ONEY IS *created by bees from nectar obtained from flowers. This is transported in the bee's crop and discharged into specially prepared cells in the bee's hive. From these honeycombs it can be harvested, most easily by centrifugal force. There is hardly any part of the world where honey is not produced. Main exporters now are Mexico, China, Argentina and Australia.*

Nearly three quarters of honey consists of inverted sugars (fructose and glucose). Its colour, taste and quality vary with the flowers from which it is collected, and with the age of the hive. Among the more common honey-producing plants are acacia, rape, clover, rosemary, orange blossom, linden or lime, thyme, eucalyptus, and heather. The first four are white, linden is greenish, heather honey dark golden.

In the ancient world honey was an important part of diet, almost the only source of sugar.

Orange blossom honey

Honeycomb

VANILLA &
ANGELICA

*V*ANILLA PLANIFOLIA *is a climbing orchid with aerial roots. Native to central American tropical forests it became important in the 19th century through French cultivation.*

The thin yellow pods, easily 6–8 inches (15–20 cm) long, are harvested unripe and part fermented, then slowly dried. Sugar packed in a jar with vanilla pods will absorb their flavour and pods can be steeped, in milk or cream then cleaned and dried for repeated use. Vanilla essence, is used in many products, from cigars to Spanish brandy and most eating chocolate contains some vanilla. In the kitchen the essence is seldom as good as pod vanilla.

Angelica *(A. Archangelica)*, a hardy biennial, grows wild throughout Northern Europe and Asia. Angelica is used in many aperitifs, is excellent with rhubarb and in marmalade. Most frequently the young stems are candied. The taste is strong and musky.

Vanilla

Angelica

G I N G E R

G INGER (ZINGIBER OFFICINALE) *is the creeping rhizome of a plant resembling the iris which originated in southeast Asia but now grows throughout the tropics.*

Ginger preserved in syrup

Candied ginger

Arab traders had introduced it to the Middle East before Roman times; the Spaniards established it in the West Indies.

Powdered ginger

Ginger can be bought preserved in syrup, candied, dried, ground to a powder (and usually adulterated), or fresh. Each form has its own use as a flavouring. Its taste is sharp and sweet at the same time, and its effect is 'hot'. In European and North American cooking ginger is widely used in baking, in drinks, and for some desserts. Hardly any country does not have its favourite gingerbread or a similar confection. Powdered ginger used to appear on the table as we now have salt and pepper. In China ginger (preserved in syrup) is eaten as a sweetmeat.

Recipes

*All recipes are for 4,
but some (such as cakes or tarts
and terrines) will serve more*

AVOCADO AND COCONUT DIP

3 oz/75 g coconut cream
2 avocados
1 small onion, chopped
1 clove garlic, sliced
2–3 green chillies, seeds removed, sliced
½ teaspoon ground cumin
salt
juice of 1 lemon
⅓ pint/200 ml plain yoghurt

Dissolve the coconut cream in ⅓ pint/200 ml water. Peel the avocados, take out the stones, and put the flesh in a blender with all the other ingredients. Blend until thoroughly liquefied. Transfer to a serving bowl, chill well and serve with toast.

By adding more water (or water and dry white wine) this dip can be turned into a delicately flavoured cold soup.

A SALAD OF COOKED PEPPERS AND TOMATOES

1 lb/500 g peppers
½ preserved lemon (page 33)
6 tablespoons olive oil
3 lb/1.5 kg tomatoes, peeled, seeded and chopped
1 clove garlic, crushed
1 teaspoon paprika
salt
a handful of chopped parsley

Grill the peppers, or scorch them over a gas flame, then put them in a paper bag or a tea towel and leave to cool. This will make it easy to remove the skins. Remove the seeds too, and dice the peppers. Discard the flesh of the lemon and dice the peel. Heat the olive oil in a heavy pan, add the tomatoes, garlic, paprika and salt. Cook gently, stirring frequently, until you have a thick tomato purée that begins to fry in the oil. Add the peppers, lemon and parsley to the pan and simmer very gently for 15 minutes, stirring frequently to prevent sticking. Leave to cool.

SMOKED HADDOCK AND ORANGE SALAD

1 large fillet of smoked haddock
¾ pint/450 ml milk
2 oranges
juice of 1 lemon
curly endive and batavia lettuce
vinaigrette

Soak the haddock in cold milk for 2 hours. Cut some long strips of zest from the oranges and put aside, then peel the fruit, removing all pith; lift the segments out of their skin and discard any pips. Drain the haddock and pat it dry. Slice it very thinly, and put the slices on a large plate. Pour over the lemon juice and scatter on the orange zest. Marinate for 15 minutes. Dress the endive and batavia with a light vinaigrette and arrange on a platter or on 4 serving plates. Put the slices of haddock on top and surround with orange segments.

PILAF WITH ALMONDS, PINE NUTS AND ORANGE PEEL

2 large oranges
12 oz/375 g Basmati rice
¼ teaspoon saffron
salt
4 oz/125 g butter
4 oz/125 g sugar
2 oz/50 g almonds, blanched and slivered
2 oz/50 g pine nuts
a good squeeze of lemon juice

Cut the peel from the oranges in narrow strips about an inch/2.5 cm long. Make sure no pith adheres to them. Put in a pan of cold water, bring to the boil, then simmer until soft. Drain, rinse well with cold water and dry.

Soak the rice in hot water for several minutes, strain, rinse and put into a pan. Dissolve the saffron in a little water, top it up to 12 fl oz/350 ml water, add salt, and pour over the rice. Bring to boiling point, then lower the heat and simmer for 10–12 minutes, until the rice is cooked but still firm.

Melt the butter in a small pan, pour half of it over the rice, cover the rice pan with a tea towel and then its lid. Turn off the heat and leave to steam for 10 minutes. The cloth will absorb the steam so the rice grains remain dry.

To the butter left in the small pan add the sugar with ¼ pint/150 ml water and cook until the sugar has dissolved. Add the orange peel, nuts and lemon juice. Simmer, stirring occasionally, until most of the water is gone and the mixture has thickened. If it dries out too fast add a little water. Mound up the rice on a heated dish, pour the nut mixture over the top and serve.

MALABAR BRAISED VEGETABLES WITH COCONUT

Most vegetables can be used for this dish, so the following is only one possible selection. Make your own, but remember to cut all vegetables to roughly the same size so that they will all cook in the same time.

1 large potato
8 oz/250 g green beans
2 peppers
6 oz/175 g shelled peas
6 oz/175 g shelled broad beans
½ teaspoon turmeric
salt
2 tomatoes
4 oz/125 g grated fresh coconut
1 teaspoon aniseed
2 cloves
seeds from 2 cardamom pods
2 hot green chillies
½ pint/300 ml plain yoghurt
2 tablespoons oil
½ teaspoon mustard seed
good pinch asafoetida

Cut up the potato, green beans and peppers and put them in a pan with the peas and broad beans and the turmeric. Cover with salted water, bring to the boil, then simmer for 7–8 minutes. Add the tomatoes, quartered; simmer for a further 3–4 minutes. Drain. Put the coconut, aniseed, cloves, cardamom seeds and chillies into a blender or food processor with ¼ pint/150 ml water and blend to a paste. Put the vegetables back in the pan together with the coconut paste and simmer, covered, for 5 minutes. Turn off the heat, stir in the yoghurt carefully, and taste for salt. Transfer to a heated serving dish.

Heat the oil and add the mustard seeds and asafoetida. When the seeds start to pop, pour the oil and spices over the vegetables and serve.

CIRCASSIAN CHICKEN

4 chicken breasts, with skin
1 onion, quartered
1 carrot, sliced thickly
1 bayleaf
a sprig of tarragon
a few black peppercorns
salt
2 slices white bread, crusts removed
1 clove garlic, crushed
pinch cayenne
2 teaspoons paprika
8 oz/250 g walnuts (or walnuts
and hazelnuts combined), ground
2 tablespoons olive oil
2 tablespoons chopped parsley

Put the chicken, onion, carrot, bayleaf, tarragon, peppercorns and a little salt in a pan, cover with water, bring to the boil, then simmer for 30 minutes until the chicken is tender. Remove it from the pan and strain the stock.

Soak the bread in a little of the stock, then transfer it to a blender or food processor together with the garlic, cayenne and half the paprika. Add ¼ pint/150 ml of the stock and blend. Add the nuts and more stock as necessary to make a thick sauce.

When the chicken is cool, remove skin and bones and cut the meat into strips. Mix well with two thirds of the sauce and spread on a serving dish, with the remaining sauce over the top.

Heat the oil in a small pan, stir in the remaining paprika and cook for a minute, then dribble the oil over the chicken. Garnish with parsley and serve at room temperature.

LAMB WITH PRESERVED LEMON

4 large lamb chops or leg cutlets
oil
2 cloves garlic
salt and pepper
1 preserved lemon (page 33)
thyme

Take 4 pieces of foil each large enough to wrap a lamb chop, and oil them lightly. Crush the garlic to a paste with a little salt and spread thinly over the lamb. Grind over some black pepper. Cut the lemon peel into thin strips and put 2 or 3 strips and a sprig of thyme on each piece of lamb. Wrap each chop tightly in the foil, put the parcels on a baking tray and cook in a slow oven, 150°C/300°F/gas 2, for 1-1½ hours.

THAI STUFFED PEPPERS

4 medium peppers, red, green or yellow
1 clove garlic
salt and pepper
1 tablespoon oil
2 tablespoons chopped coriander leaves
6 oz/175 g minced pork
6 oz/175 g prawns, chopped if large
½ teaspoon sugar
fish sauce[1], to taste
1 egg
2 tablespoons ground peanuts

Crush the garlic with a little salt and fry it in the oil for a minute or two, together with the coriander leaves. Add the pork and prawns, stir until cooked, then season to taste with pepper, sugar and fish sauce. Remove from the heat and stir in the egg and peanuts.

Cut a lid from each pepper and remove the seeds and membranes. Stuff the peppers with the mixture, replace the lids. Steam for 25–30 minutes.

1) Fish sauce, called *nam pla* in Thailand and *nuoc mam* in Vietnam, is an amber-coloured fermented sauce made from small fish and salt. It is widely used in southeast Asian cooking.

WALNUT SAUCE

4 oz/125 g walnuts
2–3 cloves garlic
salt
1 small onion, chopped finely
2 tablespoons wine vinegar
pinch ground cinnamon
pinch ground cloves
pinch cayenne
4 fl oz/125 ml water or stock
2 tablespoons chopped mint

Process the nuts with the garlic and some salt in a blender or processor. Add the onion, vinegar and spices, then enough water or stock to make a thick creamy sauce. Stir in the mint, serve at room temperature with roast chicken, baked fish, or vegetables.

SWEET AND SOUR LIME PICKLE

6 limes
2 oz/50 g salt
4 oz/125 g brown sugar
1 tablespoon ground ginger
1 tablespoon chilli powder
5 cloves
5 cardamons, lightly crushed

Cut the limes in quarters, put them in a large flat bowl, sprinkle with the salt and leave overnight. Next morning, boil the sugar and ginger with the liquid from the limes and a little water until the sugar dissolves. Stir in the chilli powder and cool. Put the limes and whole spices in a jar and pour over the syrup. Cover and keep for 4 weeks before using.

LEMON MINCEMEAT

This is based on a 19th century recipe reported by Florence White in *Good Things in England* 1932.

2 large lemons
1 lb/500 g sugar
8 oz/250 g currants
8 oz/250 g raisins, chopped
12 oz/375 g beef suet, shredded finely
pinch cloves
¼ teaspoon mace
¼ teaspoon nutmeg
3 oz/75 g candied fruits

2 oz/50 g almonds, blanched and chopped
1 or 2 glasses brandy

Wash the lemons, cut them in half, squeeze out the juice and strain it. Boil the lemon skins in several changes of water until soft enough to pound to a paste. Add the sugar to this paste and pound together. Mix in the other ingredients, adding the brandy last.

The mincemeat will keep well in closed glass jars.

PRESERVED LEMONS

A North African speciality, preserved lemons add a salty sharpness to salads and slow-cooked meats.

Take *4 or 5 lemons*, wash them well and cut them in four but not all the way through. Sprinkle *coarse salt* into the cuts, close the lemons up again and put them in a preserving jar. Press them down well and put a weight (a clean heavy stone will do) on top. In a short time juices will be released, and in a few days there should be enough to

cover the lemons. If not add a *light brine* or more *lemon juice*. Leave the lemons for a month before using. For most dishes the peel alone is used, chopped or sliced.

Baklava

An easy, rich pastry that is popular throughout the Middle East.

1 lb/500 g filo pastry
8 oz/250 g sugar
1 tablespoon lemon juice
1 tablespoon orange-flower water
6 oz/175 g unsalted butter
8 oz/250 g coarsely chopped walnuts, almonds or pistachios

Make a syrup by dissolving the sugar in ¼ pint/150 ml water with the lemon juice. Simmer until it thickens enough to coat a spoon, then stir in the orange-flower water and simmer for another minute or two. Cool and chill.

Melt the butter and use it to brush sides and bottom of a square or oblong baking tin.

Take half the sheets of filo (leaving the others wrapped) and lay them in the tin, brushing each one with butter and folding as necessary to make them fit the tin. Spread the nuts over the pastry. Cover with the remaining sheets of filo, brushing with butter and folding to fit as before. With a sharp knife cut the pastry into squares or lozenges. Bake in a preheated oven, 160°C/325°F/gas 3, for 30 minutes, then increase to 230°C/450°F/gas 8 and bake for 15 minutes more. The baklava should be crisp and puffed and light golden. Remove it from the oven and pour the chilled syrup over the hot pastry. When cold separate the pieces of pastry and serve.

Gingerbread

'Take *half a pound of almonds*, blanch and beat them till they have done shining; beat them with *a spoonful or two of orange-flower water*, put in *half an ounce of beaten ginger*, and *a quarter of an ounce of cinnamon* powdered; work it to a paste with *double refined sugar* beaten and sifted; then roll it out, and lay it on papers to dry in an oven after pies are drawn.'

E. Smith *The Compleat Housewife*, 1727

YORKSHIRE TREACLE TART

Mix together equal amounts *(say 8 oz/250 g each) brown bread crumbs* and *mixed fruit (sultanas, currants and candied peel)* with the *grated rind and juice of one lemon, a large apple (cored and grated), a pinch of ginger, a pinch of mixed spice and two tablespoons treacle.*

Grease a sandwich tin, line it with short pastry and fill with the mixture. Cover with more short pastry. Bake in a preheated oven, 200°C/400°F/gas 6, for 20–30 minutes.
Florence White, *Good Things In England*, 1932

KUMQUATS IN BRANDY

Kumquats are now widely available in the late winter months and they are very good preserved in syrup or, better still, in brandy.

1 lb/500 g kumquats
8 oz/250 g sugar
brandy

Prick each kumquat 3 or 4 times with a needle. Put the sugar in a pan with ¾ pint/450 ml water and dissolve over low heat. Turn up the heat, boil steadily for 2 minutes, then add the kumquats and simmer for 20 minutes. Drain, and reserve the syrup. Put the kumquats into warm dry jars and pour in enough brandy to come two thirds of the way up the fruit. Boil the syrup to reduce it by half, then use it to top up the jars. Cover the jars and keep for at least 2 weeks before eating.

The preserved kumquats are an excellent sweetmeat; they also go well with chocolate cakes and puddings.

FLORENTINES

4 fl oz/125 ml double cream
2 oz/50 g caster sugar
2 oz/50 g ground almonds
2 oz/50 g blanched flaked almonds
*2 oz/50 g crystallized orange peel,
chopped finely*
1 oz/25 g angelica
1 oz/25 g flour
pinch salt
4 oz/125 g plain chocolate

Heat the cream and sugar until
the sugar melts, then stir in the
almonds, orange peel, angelica,
flour and salt, in that order.
Grease and flour a baking tray
and drop teaspoons of the
mixture onto it, leaving room
for the biscuits to spread. Bake
in a preheated oven, 180°C/
350°F/gas 4, for 12 minutes.
Leave the biscuits to cool
slightly before removing them
from the tray.
Melt the chocolate in a bowl
over simmering water and cool
to lukewarm. With a palette
knife spread chocolate over the
bottoms of the biscuits and
leave them to stand until the
chocolate is firm.

ALMOND CREAM

'Take *a quart of cream*, boil it
with *half a nutmeg* grated, and
a blade or two of mace, and *a bit
of lemon-peel*, and sweeten it to
your taste; then blanch *a
quarter of a pound of almonds*,
beat them very fine with *a
spoonful of rose or orange-flower
water*, take the *whites of nine eggs*
well beat, and strain them over
your almonds, beat them
together, and rub them very
well through a hair-sieve, mix
all together with your cream,
set it on the fire, stir it all one
way all the time till it boils,
pour it into your cups or
dishes, and when it is cold
serve it up.'

Hannah Glasse, *The Art of
Cookery, Made Plain and Easy,*
1747

CHOCOLATE SEMI-FREDDO

3 eggs
2 oz/50 g sugar
1/2 pint/300 ml single cream or milk
5 oz/150 g bitter chocolate
seeds from 3 cardamom pods
1/4 pint/150 ml double cream

Beat together the egg yolks and the sugar. Heat the cream or milk, pour it into the mixture while stirring. Heat in a double boiler or over a pan of simmering water until the custard thickens enough to coat the back of a spoon. Remove from the heat.

Melt the chocolate in a bowl over a pan of simmering water. Mix into the custard together with the cardamom seeds and leave to cool.

Whisk the eggs whites to stiff peaks. Lightly whip the cream. Fold both into the cold custard mixture, pour into a soufflé dish and freeze. Serve straight from the freezer.

VANILLA ICE CREAM

1 pint/600 ml single cream
1 vanilla pod or 1 teaspoon vanilla extract
4 egg yolks
4 oz/125 g sugar

Heat the cream gently with the vanilla pod or extract. When boiling point is reached, remove from heat, cover the pan and leave to infuse for 10 minutes.

Beat the yolks and sugar until thick and pale. Remove the vanilla pod, pour the cream slowly onto the yolks, whisking as you do so. Put the mixture into a double boiler and heat, stirring all the while, until the custard is thick enough to coat the back of a spoon. Cool, then either pour it straight into an ice cream machine or add praline (page 39) or cassata, mixture (page 39), and freeze according to the manufacturer's instructions.

GINGER ICE CREAM

3 egg yolks
3 oz/75 g light brown sugar
½ pint/300 ml milk
3–4 pieces preserved ginger, chopped
finely
2 tablespoons ginger syrup
3 tablespoons amontillado sherry
¼ pint/150 ml double or whipping
cream

Whisk the egg yolks and sugar together until the mixture is thick and pale. Whisk in the milk and put the mixture in a double boiler (or the mixing bowl over a pan of simmering water) and heat, stirring constantly, until the mixture is thick enough to coat the back of a spoon. Do not let it boil, or it will curdle.

Remove from the heat, stir in the ginger, syrup and sherry. Leave to cool, then whip the double cream to soft peaks and fold it into the custard. Pour into an ice cream machine and freeze according to the manufacturer's instructions.

HONEY ICE CREAM

¾ pint/450 ml double cream
5 oz/150 g orange blossom honey
2 tablespoons orange-flower water
grated rind of 1 orange

Whip the cream to soft peaks, then fold in the honey, orange-flower water and orange rind. Put into a shallow container and freeze until firm.

CASSATA

Soak *2 tablespoons* each of finely chopped *candied peel, sultanas,* finely chopped *angelica* and slivered *blanched almonds* in *2 tablespoons brandy* for about an hour. Add this mixture to *vanilla ice cream* (page 37) just before it goes into the ice cream machine.

PRALINE

Boil *4 oz/125 g sugar* with *2 tablespoons of water* until it turns golden brown. Remove from the heat and add *6 oz/175 g blanched and toasted almonds*, stirring so that they become coated with the syrup. Pour the mixture onto an oiled baking tray and leave to cool and set, then crush or coarsely grind it.

Stored in a screw-top jar the praline will keep for several weeks.

It is an excellent flavouring for cakes and ice creams. The vanilla ice cream on page 37 could have 6 oz/175 g praline added to it just before freezing.

ICED NOUGAT

4 egg whites
2 oz/50 g sugar
4 oz/125 g honey
3/4 pint/450 ml double cream
4 tablespoons whisky
2 oz/50 g sultanas
2 oz/50 g candied citrus peel, chopped finely
1 oz/25 g angelica, chopped finely
4 oz/125 g walnuts and/or hazelnuts, chopped
6 oz/175 g praline (opposite)

Whisk the egg whites to stiff peaks. Heat the sugar and honey carefully and as they come to boiling point pour the mixture into the egg whites. Stir continuously for 5 minutes.

Whip the cream, add the whisky and fold in the egg mixture. Stir in the fruit and nuts, put the mixture in a terrine or soufflé dish and freeze for at least 6 hours.

To turn out the nougat, dip the bottom of the dish in hot water and slide a knife around the edge. Sprinkle thickly with the praline and serve.

INDEX

ACKNOWLEDGEMENTS

*The publishers
would like to thank the
following people:*

· ILLUSTRATORS ·
JANE THOMSON
SHEILAGH NOBLE

JACKET
· PHOTOGRAPHY ·
PHILIP DOWELL

· MARBLER ·
SARAH AMATT

FALKINER FINE
PAPERS LTD

· TYPESETTING ·
WYVERN
TYPESETTING LTD

· REPRODUCTION ·
COLOURSCAN
SINGAPORE